Why Everyone's Fleeing Britain

Hamed Yaser

Published by Hamed Yaser, 2025.

While every precaution has been taken in the preparation of this book, the publisher assumes no responsibility for errors or omissions, or for damages resulting from the use of the information contained herein.

WHY EVERYONE'S FLEEING BRITAIN

First edition. April 30, 2025.

Copyright © 2025 Hamed Yaser.

ISBN: 979-8231480388

Written by Hamed Yaser.

Making it. Not making it. Financial prosperity. The societal pressure to look legit. The desperation to keep your head above water and put your entire focus on just surviving. Or, that last breath you take before checking out. Which are you? Thought so! Yeah, many of us out there are just trying to survive each passing day as painlessly as possible and as gracefully as possible. I am not talking about those of us who are already under the water and drowning, just talking about the ones we hopelessly call "the lucky ones". Alright, without further ado let's go ahead and get started on what we are trying to accomplish here. I would like to introduce myself and tell you what I do and how I can help you. No! I am not collaborating with BetterHelp.com or commercial help channels like that. Now I do believe in therapy and how it sets you on the path of recovery, but this book is not about therapy. Sit tight and listen up, then decide if you want my help:

My name is Amanda Hustler, and I really am a hustler. I am 28 years old, female, single, smart, go getter, with a loving touch. My close friends call me "Amanda the butcher" but what they really mean is "Amanda the knocker". I knock on the doors of strangers' homes and ask if they want my service. No! I am not a cleaner, housekeeper, Plummer, roofer, or any of that; you would not want me cleaning or fixing your home because I can really ruin your entire house and leave like nothing happened. I offer my service to most of you out there and it's making you look good and feel good about yourself, temporarily of course because if you want to feel good about yourself permanently you`ll need to work on yourself and that is when you take advantage of therapy and counselling to better yourself. My service has temporary results so there goes the disclaimer and I hope you understand the reality of being the only one in control of your happiness. Nobody is coming and therefore you must lose hope, so you feel better about life in general. You can live with the darkest realities knowing they are real, but you cannot live with the brightest doubts even when they seem so promising so quit daydreaming all together, it doesn't go far enough to make it worthwhile. I do not give people false hope, I give them temporary satisfaction about what they have and please notice that I did not say "who they are"; it is almost an impossibility to make people feel good about who they are, the best you can do is make them feel great about their attainments. This comes to many as a disappointment since the goal in life is surely not to accumulate attainments because down the road those attainments will not be of much help to you. Old white men (well mostly them) work themselves like martyrs of capitalism, then when they get older (fifty plus year olds) things are on the downward spiral. That's when these older men start looking for something beyond what they accumulated and the money they have saved in their 401K retirement accounts: authentic human connection. Lack of authentic human connection which could also be defined as loneliness kills your spirit before killing your body. Loneliness exacerbates certain mental and physiological illnesses such as dementia and shatters morals no matter who you are. Actually, there are exceptions to this rule as I know there are people out there who never need company and they absolutely thrive without any human connection whatsoever. There could be psychological reasons behind it and me not being a psychologist, I cannot confirm whether those people are actually considered normal or healthy, so we leave them out for now respectfully. There have been studies that show loneliness can be as dangerous as smoking a bunch of cigarettes a day, so anytime I hear people say there were lonely so they sought help, I root for them and congratulate them on taking steps in making progress towards a healthier life. Problem is everybody wants an easy way out of misery and unhappiness, a pill, a tiny little pill to swallow and watch as their loneliness drifts away from them; there are pills out there for depression and other mental illnesses but they are temporary solution to modern human's problem of loneness. So are the services I offer; they give you temporary satisfaction but never contentment with life. I hope you don't suspect my services are a scam or here I am trying to take

WHY EVERYONE'S FLEEING BRITAIN

advantage of vulnerable people when they are at their lowest point in life. My goal and intention is to allow people to feel what generally content people feel everyday of their life and really get a perspective on how life can be pink and peachy if they change their circumstances. Sometimes people need to see what they are missing to get motivated and start moving the muscles that haven't been put to work for a long time. In working with these sad and discontent people, I realized that often we need to see what life is going to be like once we get to the other side, some people can use their imagination to get a sense of that amazing feeling and some need my help. That is what I do: I help people what it feels like to get to the other side of darkness and start experiencing life in a different way, a more beautiful way.

Life has its ups and downs so don't assume because you are currently in a good place and are enjoying and living your best life, you won't ever need my help. Many of my clients used to think they had it all and were in a good spot, until they realized it was just their delusion making them think they were all well. A lot of times I get these older white men, those who are believed to be the most privileged of all in the society we live in, and I am shocked by how empty and pitiful their life is. These older white men have money, security, respect, family, and everything else a human being needs to live a comfortable life, but they lack what a good life requires: purpose! You heard me right, we all need to have a purpose in life to give us a direction, a goal, and a motive to get up every morning, without it there is no meaning to life. Sure, you can have a family and provide for them but then your children grow out of your nest and move on with their life and lead a different path for themselves. Your kids can allow you to be a part of their lives, but that won't be enough for you to carry on and push through emptiness of your soul and the misery life brings upon every live being on this planet. We must find a legit purpose, something that comes with solid responsibility and a sense of belonging. Funny story: I once read a book that was telling a story about how a bunch of young women were sent to jail to serve time for something relating to political activities against the regime of their country. When they were in prison they had this circle of support, they supported one another no matter what, and through hardship formed this invincible bond and sisterhood that they fed off for as long as they were in prison. When they released finally, after five or six years, they went off their individual life and soon realized they were much happier in prison. One of them goes to a therapist to get help and tells her therapist she had a much happier life in prison and three months after being released from prison, once the hype of freedom was over, she realized she was not as happy as she was in prison. The therapist asked her some questions, and at the end the therapist told her she was happier in prison because she had a purpose when she was locked up in that tiny cell: Freedom! She agreed and said that she had so many plans for when she got out, going to the movies, going to the park, partying till late at night, kissing men, falling in love, and much more. However, three months after being released and set free in the real world, she learned that none of those things brought her much happiness or satisfaction and that the idea of doing those things were pleasing not actually doing them; not even falling in love in reality was what she thought it would be.

The point I'm trying to make here is that no matter what the circumstances, we are always in need of a purpose to carry on and to make something of ourselves. I have seen people whose kids battled childhood cancer and deal with the worst of the worst: watching life getting yanked out of your child. I cannot fathom how they feel and how they deal with their emotions watching their kids decline, something that just kills your morale. To my surprise, these incredible parents move mountains and push through the pain for one reason: To help their child get through their most terrifying event in life and ease their pain. These parents are motivated by a strong purpose and inspired by their children's strength. You need a purpose to keep living, do not think that you can get through life without a purpose. I do believe, however, that you can live for some time without a purpose, but once the forbearance period is over you must find a purpose to carry on and make it to the end.

The suicide rate in Europe is at an all-time high. Why is that? Don't these successful European countries provide for their citizens and give them social support when needed? Don't these countries have the lowest rate of poverty? Why do their citizens commit suicide when they've got it all? Lack of sunshine, yes! But that cannot be the only reason why people take their own life. Now, there has been research done on this subject as it is extremely serious and sensitive. I know the research points out the importance of having meaningful relationships and being socially active, but how about having a strong purpose in life to work towards? If your life is so comfortable and your government is taking good care of you, which reduces stress, of course, then would that leave you with enough desire and motivation to make something of yourself? I must say that a lot of successful Nordic European countries have taken the motivation away from their citizens by providing for them what the citizens could have provided for themselves by hard work and pushing through hardships. Having to make ends meet keeps you on your toes and gives you a strong sense of purpose in life. I have met lots of poor people here in the States who worked two or three jobs so they could send their kids to a better school and so their children could have a better education than they did.

Now, back to where we were: why do those older white men suffer in life when they have everything an average human being would want to have in life? I personally would have stopped working if I had everything these older men have and probably wouldn't be writing these books either which is shocking because you would think that I love writing. I do love writing, it has been a dream of mine to write a book and now I have written four books, published and purchased by people who like reading my stuff. If I had enough money to feel secure in life, I probably would not have got out of bed, let alone write. I think you need to have that insecurity in life, enough of it but not too much, to cultivate and nurture your skills and talents. The need to make money gives you stress, and stress triggers these hidden talents to come up to the surface where they get attention and are then nurtured to turn into something you can make money off.

I write because I have found writing to south my soul and it also helps me make extra money that I might want to spend on candy, donuts and other things I don't need but want. What if I had rich parents who provided for me all along and I didn't need to lift a figure? Would I still be writing today? Or I would just go out for expensive lunches with fake friends and then have a coffee run? To be plainly honest, I do not know what I would do if I had lots of money to spare. I have never been in a situation where money was not an issue, I mean since adulting because I had a very comfortable life when I lived with my parents. As soon as I left home, and I started adulting, things changed, and I realized I had to watch my spending and budget my money, hard earned money.

Now, looks like the demographic where most of my customers belong to, are the most advantaged and yet they need my help to make them feel better about themselves. There are of course others from other demographic groups who ask for my help and they have their own story.

In this book I will be telling you stories about my customers, people who pay me big bucks to make them feel better.

Here is the question you are yearning for me to answer: What service do you offer? And what do you mean by making them feel better about themselves?

I act as people's ugly half. I show them what it's like to be on the other side and have the things they don't have, or don't have the things they have. I act as if I want to be them even when they are the most miserable people on the fact of this planet. I make it look like I envy them, and sometimes jealous of them even though I would never want to be in their shoes. I start with putting myself in their shoes to see through what lenses they see the world and most importantly their lives and their circumstances. This allows me to observe and learn what is bothering them the most and what is bringing them the most joy. I then look carefully to see how they want others to treat them and what they want from those around them. Once I have all this information, I proceed to planning for how I am going to present myself to them, so they get exactly what they want out of my friendship/acquaintanceship. Next up comes my magic, what I get paid for, and what I give my heart and soul to: Treating my clients how they wish to be treated so they can feel what they want to feel.

The stories I am going to tell you are selections of the most memorable clients I had. I mean these are not the worst clients or the most demanding clients, but just the ones that stood out to me and I like to see them as the unique clients I served. Now, if you are ready let's sit tight and get started.

Cody – The invisible man

"Why don't you have presence, Cody? Why not tell the world that you are here"

I was in my own zone when I heard a knock on my door, pizza time! I opened the door and grabbed the two pizzas the delivery guy had left at my door and quickly closed the door. I love pizza and sometimes I just feel like I have an addiction to pizza which is perhaps destroying my body and health. I like to order pizza sometimes when I work late at night so in a way I have rewarded myself with the kind of food I love. I mean, don't get me wrong, I like my own cooking too which is why 90 percent of the time I cook for myself and baby girl but sometimes I just need to try somebody's else's cooking too. I opened the first box of pizza, oh my Gosh, the smell hit my face and I fell in love instantly, I grabbed a piece and ate it. Love, Love, Love! I looked at my baby girl staring at me wondering why I wasn't sharing my food with her, and gave her a piece too. She didn't like it and ate only a little bit then left the rest for me to finish, as if I was going to eat her left over pizza. I like to either watch something or do something when I`m eating so I stood behind my work desk and kept typing words, oh yes, I eat standing up, it's my way of enjoying food. My baby girl kept sniffing the pizza boxes and once noticed it's the same food she didn't like, she left and laid down on the sofa. Now, Cody! What was up with our boy, Cody who did not want to exist, of course not the way most people would imagine, no not like that; Cody did not want to have presence when in a crowd or group. Unfortunately, that was the case around his family and close friends too. He was usually in his own mind and did not mind people not noticing him anyway so he would just keep quiet and listen. He was mostly a spectator standing in the corner and not having the will or desire to join in the conversation. I couldn't figure just by that one meeting we had if he had an avoidant personality disorder or was just shy. Well, I have to admit, I do not have a degree in psychology and maybe I'm not qualified to even make a call on what is going on with people in terms of their mental health. Cody reminded me of a college back in a day when I worked at that boring corporate job I had; I think that guy's name was Brock, yes it was Brock indeed. I remember a lot of times we would actually forget Brock existed even though he was right there sitting next to us in meetings, gatherings, working sessions, and his cubicle was even right next to me. On Fridays when we were curious to see who had come to work and walked around the office, we would see Brock but it's like his presence wouldn't count. My coworkers and I were never actually mean or unkind to Brock, it's just that we didn't know if he even wanted to be counted in. Sometimes we would invite him to our gatherings and celebrations, just to realize we had made him extremely uncomfortable by inviting him. He genuinely enjoyed his own company and solitude and I respected him for that knowing that a lot of people cannot stand themselves for more than a couple of minutes and constantly have to be in presence of others just to survive life.

With Cody, I thought I needed to dig a bit deeper to see if there were underlying issues that made him shrink himself and seek invisibility when in presence of others. I had an idea of why he was seeking not to be seen: the fear of criticism and even rejection by his peers. Parents often play the major role in planting the seed of fear in their beloved children, most of the time unknowingly and out of their undeniable love for them, instead of giving the nurturing safe zone to be comfortable in their own skin, why not? Because, parents are human too and they make irreversible mistake causing damages that can no longer be fixed. Sometimes when I meet people like Cody, I think for some people it may have been better to be raised like Tarzan in the jungle away from toxic care givers or even narcissus parents. Tarzan perhaps was the lucky child who got to be himself and do what he wanted to do without the constant criticism of others around him.

I started day dreaming about Tarzan and got to work. I had to finish up writing Cody's scenarios for our next session so we could get to work and do something good for Cody. I ate the entire pizza and only left a couple of pieces for my dinner. Oh, yes I do have a huge stomach that can take in lots of food but that day for some reason my stomach did feel a bit uncomfortable with that much food in it all at once.

The next morning, I realized I needed one more meeting with Cody before our sessions officially started and so I texted him and asked if we could meet over a coffee or something. He responded right away saying he was free that afternoon and if I could make then, it would be great. I was conveniently free that afternoon and so I texted him back saying I was happy to meet him at Nerd's Café at 5 in the afternoon.

"I am so glad you could make time for me. I really need to talk to you about your childhood as it could have had the most effect on you not wanting to have a strong presence. So, can you tell me a little about your childhood? Also, I understand a Café may not be the best place to discuss such sort of things so let me know if you like to go to my office."

"No, I`m ok talking about my childhood here in the café. Do you want me to start from when I was born?"

"Yes, please!"

"My parents were both extremely religious and believed we all have to suffer in this world so we can go to heaven. It's stupid and I do not want to have anything to do with that sort of beliefs. I knew deep down, always, that these are non-sense beliefs that holds a strong grip on people who are not mentally strong enough to deal with the reality of life as is. I hated everything about my religious parents and it's shameful to talk about them like that but I have to be honest here, right? So, I grew up in a small town where people had nothing to do other than gossiping behind each other's back and I wanted nothing to do with that either. I remember just studying really hard to get into a college outside of that ugly town and well, hard work paid off and I got admitted into Stanford University in California with full scholarship. I liked college, made lots of friends who were genuinely interested in spending time with me and I also met this really cute girl, Angela, who I dated for three years. My college years were the best; I had a sense of purpose and was looking forward to graduating and maybe meeting my girlfriend's parents. Shortly after I graduated my girl got a job in another state and moved leaving me behind kind of. The year of 2011 was not the best year to be job hunting as the economy had not yet recovered but I did not lose hope. I kept searching and searching, and when I was convinced my engineering degree was not going to get me an entry level engineer position, I decided to put my pride aside and apply for internships anywhere in the state of California where I wanted to live. After 6 grueling months of job hunting, I finally landed a temporary engineering internship at an aerospace company and was unbelievably proud of myself to have landed a job in that economy. People in that company liked me and kept complementing me on how hard I worked and little spoke. They were often puzzled by why I was so quiet but really didn't mind me not talking as middle aged men and women took care of the talking part. Life seemed to be going for me, but then as my career took off my personal life took a dip and from there I kept getting more and more isolated and lonely. I had already lost my college girl friend since I decided not to do long distance relationship and could not seem to get a girl. At work my boss tried to hook me up with girls but they were so difficult to please or were too immature to be in a relationship with. There was this one girl, I think she was middle-eastern, who I really enjoyed talking to and we did go out a few times as friends hiking and things like that but she didn't like me like that. I was so disappointed that she didn't like me that I wanted to leave that company and just put myself in a different environment to refresh my mindset. As the time went on, and I got older, things just got more and more complicated and dating got dreadful. I eventually gave up on dating but still hope to find the one."

"Ok, thank you for sharing your life story with me. I wanted to hear your life story because essentially I need to know what your background is and what really got you here. I mean where you are is pretty stable and solid, but it seems like you don't believe you are living your best life. Is that right?"

"Yes, it maybe that I haven't found the one, you know? I need to find my soul mate and being too withdrawn and avoidant, I cannot find the right girl for me."

"Having a soul mate is great! But, we have to be whole before finding our better half so the relationship can work for both of us. Having a partner is supposed to be food, to fill you up and give you the energy you need to achieve what you want in life, but it's not supposed to be medicine to fight your internal demons."

"You described it really well. Yeah, I should not take my future romantic partner as medication and just food."

"There you go. But, you know Cody what worries me the most, is the fact that you tend to avoid people and if they push you, you seem to be pull back even harder. I can understand you doing that when don't like an individual, but when you do it with everybody then that's a different story. When listening to your life story I was looking for hints of when or where this avoidance strategy came into play and I think it's really how your parents treated you when you were much too young to even understand what is going on around you. Your parents used punishment as a mean to enforce their rules at home, and that made you isolate to avoid getting punished because you didn't know what you were doing that was wrong. In your innocent mind, you had done nothing wrong and just the fact that you couldn't make sense of why you were getting punished made you fearful of being around your parents. Later in life that translated into avoiding any kind of relationship where there needed to be specific rules and agreements

WHY EVERYONE'S FLEEING BRITAIN

with your partner out of fear or getting punished. The reason I'm saying all this is because we need to look at the root of the problem and I can help with seeing how good life is going to be once you take care of the main issue, but you have to make an intention for yourself to seek therapy after our sessions. My sessions will show you the end result, once you are done with professional help and therapy and I am here to show you that the other side maybe greener. After you see the other side, and decide to take a leap and change your life, every move you need to make to get to the other side will appear right in front of you."

Why do I never tell people that it's all going to be OK one day? Well, what if that one day is the day they check out of this world? I mean how would I know when they day was going to arrive? I sometimes, badly want to tell my clients that everything is going to be OK if they seek help and go to therapy and talk to a professional who knows how to direct them to the right path, the path of healing and inner peace. At the end of the day it all depends on how my clients take their next steps towards and if you ask me I say it is so difficult to make all the decisions by yourself and be held responsible had that decision proven to be wrong. You pay a hefty price for being an adult and it's the kind of price that doesn't buy you a whole lot of happiness; yet another reason for why I do not want children and will not bring another human being to suffer in this world.

My invisible man was right, not being seen was a way out that almost guaranteed no annoyance at least from the others who may or may not have bad intentions. Maybe that's the answer to adults' problems, to avoid being around people as much as you can afford you. Lately I have been thinking being invisible and having solitude is what divides the rich from the poor. You know what I mean? I wish life did not have to be so exhausting for people, it is at times exhausting for me as well but somehow I bounce back, and what if bouncing back and getting back to where you left off is too painful for some. It always baffles me when under privileged people have children, how selfish is that? If you suffer in this world, chances are your children will suffer as well and how can you want that for another being as fragile and sensitive as a child? No, God did not build this world well and he knows that too well.

After going through an episode of existential dread, I got up, made some coffee and stood behind my desk ready to start working on Cody's case. In a way I felt guilty about pulling Cody out of his comfort zone knowing he was so cocooned in his own warmth, but I had to do what he had asked me to do: Show him the other side.

I worked on his case for about an hour and then did some editing and re-assessing. What I had put together for him was pretty good, I just had to look over one last time to be sure of my plan for Cody. Once I finished my work, I walked to over to the living room to see what my dog was doing, and as always I found my love sleeping peacefully on the sofa. Her eyes were moving, I could tell they were moving even though they were shut closed, so I guess she was dreaming. I read somewhere that dogs dream about their owners, my heart just melted.

"Hi, Cody.... I just wanted to give you heads up that I have finished up your plan. Are you free next week, maybe Tuesday?"

"Sure, Tuesday sounds good. That was fast. I thought it was going to take you much longer to put that plan together but I guess you are pretty good at what you do."

"Yup, I have enough experience to be able to compile everything as soon as needed. I'll see you Tuesday then!"

It feels great when your clients compliment you on how good you are at what you do. Cody was a nice man and I was glad he gave me a few compliments since we met. I was ready to work with him to see what I could potentially learn from the quiet young man.

"So here is the scenario I put together for you, please take a look and let me know if you have any questions. I just want to warn you that the things you are about to read may not be too comfortable for you to say out loud or play. I want you to know that we are trying to get you to play the person you want to become, so just try to go with the flow and don't take things personal. Does that sound OK?"

"Yeah, well it may be too hard to not take things personal but I'm not sure if I'll really mold into this new character. I'll try."

"Trying is good enough. Let's go! Oh Hi, Cody.... OMG, haven't seen you for a while, how have you been?"

"Yeah, been great. I actually been terrific lately, I have started my own business which is something I always wanted for me and now I have finally done it."

"That is wonderful, what kind of a business is that if I may ask?"

"Yeah, it's basically an IT consultation company focusing on cyber security. I have about 50 people working for me and it's such a great accomplishment for me, having worked for a corporation that treated its employees like dirt and worked like a dog for years. You know I am just taking over the world, oh, that's how it feels like at least."

"You must be proud of yourself, not just what you achieved but having the drive to get 50 people under your wing and treating them well, paying them well, and not working them to death. You have become a leader, not a boss and that is what's impressive with you."

"Yeah, I always wanted to guide people to do what's best for them. I tell my employees that they can leave the job whenever they want to pursue their dream or just get a higher paying job. I don't want to be a boss, I always wanted to be the one who inspires people, the one who people look up to and hold up to higher standards. I have become that person and now I have more power to even have greater impact. My employees watch my every move and put me under microscope monitoring my actions to see how I got to where I am today and that is so satisfying."

"Is it the money you make or the influence you have over people that's most satisfying about having a successful business?"

"It's all of it. I love standing on the top of the mountain and have people watch me do my job. I enjoy being followed by people who work for me, they are great people and deserve to reach success like I did. I want what I have for all of them and that's why I'm helping them grow. I did my time in a corporate environment and will never create an atmosphere that feels as greedy as it did in corporations."

"What do people do to become you?"

"They just have to be open to new ideas and challenging themselves, going outside their comfort zone and taking risks, like I did. Ever risk I took, it was extremely uncomfortable, I felt like I wasn't built to have what I was striving for but after working in that dead end job I realized life is too meaningless not to try risky things. Without intriguing actions, life is too dull to live."

"But, a lot of people are too afraid of the judgment of the others if they fail. Did you fear that?"

"Well, at first yes, but then I kept assuring myself that I could do what I put my entire focus on, and that I was built to achieve higher than my own expectations if I was ok with paying the price, of course."

"So, what is the price of success?"

"Missing out of normal activities. That is the biggest price you have to be willing to pay to have something of your own, a business, something you are proud of and have sacrificed so much of your youth for."

"Well done, Cody! You did great today, I'm so proud of you."

Are all clients of mine as cooperative as Cody or do I have more difficult clients at times that challenge me real good? I like Cody for who he is and I think deep down he knows that. Even though he likes to be invisible and shaded, he knows he is very likable and that people would want to be his friend just because Cody has a very personable character and is generously kind too. I needed to talk to Cody a bit more to get a more thorough understanding of his mental health. Typically, people don't hide from the others for no good reason. Even when they go into hiding because they just claim to need some space, one needs to understand what that space provide for them that being with others does not. Usually, we are supposed to feel secure around others and that is how normal people feel, but then when you were hurt as a child you seek distance and avoidance to gain that security. Meaning, you seek the opposite of what a normal person would seek to get security and safety. The way I saw Cody's situation was that, he was a very sensitive person and therefore he did not have that thick skin that you would need to deal with criticism. This could be the reason for why he did not want to be seen so nobody could call him out for any wrong doing he may do. I see this as insecurity, a protective act to avoid life threatening situations and keep sane. My heart started acing for poor Cody, how bad of a childhood did this guy endure?

"Hi, Cody.... I feel like our last session went really well. How did you feel about it?"

"I felt awkward. That's it. Do you even think this is going to work? I sense that I'm just playing something that is not going to work and it makes me feel pathetic, and dumb. I mean after we finished our session I went home and took a shower, and the entire time I was in the shower I could not bare to look myself in the mirror. Why is that? Because I was ashamed of myself. I was ashamed of pretending to be wanting to be the center of attention and worst of all, enjoying myself getting attention. I don't want to play this game anymore."

"I hear you, Cody! I do. The reason I wanted to meet with you again and talk is because deep down I feel like we need to do some therapy here."

"Therapy? I thought you said your services are not like therapy and that you are not even a licensed therapist."

"Correct! I am not a therapist and do not do therapy as part of my normal work. But, I want you to know that at this point, it seems like we need to dig a bit deeper to get to the root cause of your issues. It is a critical part of my work that I understand what is broken inside of you, so I know how to proceed further. My hope is that we get to the root of your issues and steer in the right direction."

"I'm glad that you are so optimistic about fixing me up. I'm afraid I am not up for it, maybe it's just not time for me to make such drastic change to my life. However, I am willing to go with what you say and what you decide for me. For once, I just want to be in the passenger seat."

"Cody, you are on the driver seat! You are the one in control and I am only suggesting where to go and what to do, you are still in control of everything in your life. Now, I like to ask you some questions if that is OK with you. Were you treated harshly by your parents? I don't mean your parents criticizing you in front of the others. I mean did they physically mistreat you?"

"I was going to lie and tell you that my parents never laid hands on me, but why should I keep lying about things that hurt me the most? I am not going to lie anymore, I am tired of lying to myself and others. My parents abused me physically and left me with deep emotional scars that have taken me to an excruciatingly dark and lonely place. I need help."

"I hear you, Cody! I do! I want to help you find peace and contentment which is why I wanted to talk more with you to get to the bottom of why you seek solitude. I can now see why that is."

"I cannot believe I actually talked about the abuse I endured when I was young. I never talk about what happened to me when I was a child. I guess it takes a great deal of vulnerability to get naked so a stranger can see your wounds."

"That is the hardest part when you are on the recovery path. Now, can we talk about how long this physical abuse lasted?"

"Until I was fourteen or fifteen, that's when it all stopped, mainly because I was old enough to defend myself and my parents no longer dared to hit me. The last time my dad laid his hands on me, I got up and held his arm as it was coming down on me and I told my dad that if he ever tries to hit me again, I will hit him back and I will hit him much harder than he ever hit me. I knew then, that my parents were no longer my protector and that they would do anything to destroy me. I was furious with them, and they were hateful towards me. It just goes to show that not every parent deserves a child but every child deserves a parent. I was so badly abused by my parents, my mother never protected me against my father and just stood there and watched, I don't know how she felt about me getting beaten by my dad but she didn't seem to be bothered by it. I sometimes, feel like I hate her a lot more than I hate my dad, I mean she is a mother and mothers are supposed to be the ultimate protectors of their offerings. I knew I had to leave home as soon as I could and so I started working very young and saved up my money to move out. And, that's what I did. The best day of my life was when I got my own apartment and started a new life on my own, it really was the best day of my life away from my abusers. Of course, my parents tried to find me and texted me several times after I left. One time my mother pleaded with me to go back home because she was missing me so much, but I knew, they had probably plotted something evil against me. I was smart enough not to return home and basically continue working and making money. I feel great about where I am today in life, but need to become comfortable with myself and others. Do you think you can help me?"

"Are you kidding? Of course, I can help you. I have a better understanding of what happened to you when you were a child. Did you ever try to report your parents' abuse?"

"I guess that was my shortcoming. No, I never did and I don't know how bad the abuse should have gotten for me to realize that I need to report my parents so they would get the punishment they badly deserved. They should have gone to jail for years but I just didn't have the guts to report those disgraceful people. I sort of hate myself for not doing the right thing."

"Don't hate yourself. You don't even know how your parents would have reacted had you reported them to the police. My belief is that with abusive parents, it is extremely tricky finding the best course of action, especially when you are so young and vulnerable. I am actually really proud of what you accomplished at such a young age, working jobs and making money. Let's just say that a lot of young people do not have the drive or motivation to do all the work you did to have independence, and I applaud you for it."

"Life is strange. I wish I had an easier life so I could relax a bit."

"Going back to our sessions...now, I like to put together a different scenario for you to play. This time around we may want to go back to your childhood and do some sessions around the damages you incurred when you were young. I hope you trust me with that."

"I do. I guess at this point I just want to heal my wounds and move on. I don't want to be stuck in my childhood and the things that happened when I had no control of whatsoever."

Did Cody remind me of myself when I was young and hapless? I did not have bad parents, they did not abuse me or hit me. My parents were OK just not supportive or kind toward me and mostly critical of me. Cody's words were heart wrenching, they actually burnt my wounds or maybe his words opened up my old wounds and then burnt them. As a child, I felt neglected and mostly disliked by my parents and tried everything I could think of to get my parents attention which mostly ended up in some kind of annoyance from my parents. How much can a child take at such a tender age? I wish my parents were more attentive to me and showed me that they loved me. They did love me, but their actions poorly reflected their feelings toward me. I am sorry to any child who longs for attention and never gets it. I think part of the reason I don't want children is because of my own experiences as a child who was neglected most of the time.

I needed to distract myself from my evil thoughts that ate me alive, so I turned to my baby girl and started talking to her. She tilted her head which made her extra adorable and I couldn't take it anymore so I ran to her and gave her a huge hug. She was a little uncomfortable me holding her so tightly to my chest and so she pulled back and tried to free herself from me. I let her go since I didn't want to hurt her feelings. I came back to my senses at the sound of email notification. I checked my phone and noticed I had a new client. Wow, my business was taking off and looks like the prospect of growing my business was becoming a real thing. I was definitely proud of what I had created, all on my own, things were flowing the direction I wanted them to and it was the path of least resistance. I knew leaving my corporate job was the best thing I could have ever done and it was the right move for someone who could not tolerate office politics and the meaninglessness of a 9 to 5 job. My old coworkers have been contacting me asking how I`m doing and whether I regret leaving that high paying job and my answer is always: "I wish I left way earlier."

After patting myself on the back, I proceeded to make some afternoon coffee so I could start working on Cody's case. I am so lucky to make money while actually helping people bring joy to their life. The coffee tasted not too nice but still drinkable. I sat down and started working on a new scenario for Cody. I worked for over six hours and right when my eyes started burning like hell, I stopped working and started contemplating dinner since it had already past lunch time. I felt like McDonalds for some reason and so I ordered through Doordash. There is this great feeling when you are waiting for your food to arrive and continue working, it's like these really serious business people who make others prepare their meal while they focus on more important work. Haha, sounds ridiculous!!! What work is more important than food? Doordash track showed I had about 25 minutes to work before my food arrived so I tried to get whatever I could done so after dinner I could just relax. I got Cody's case to a good place and was confident I would complete it before the end of the week, I just had to doge a few lazy episodes I was going to encounter during the next few days. The dinner arrived and I got busy stuffing my mouth with my fish sandwich and some awful fries.

After finishing Cody's case, I reached out to him and told him that I was ready to go through the scenario I had put together for him. Cody responded immediately and said that he was looking forward to meeting with me. Nice! I was on the right track.

"Thank you, Cody, for meeting with me again. This time we are going to try another scenario where you are not going to be enjoying attention, instead you will be assured that you are loved every time you do something wrong. Don't worry if you don't connect right away, just go with the flow and let this scenario take you to a safe place. There is no judgment here."

"Hi, Cody... Thanks for meeting with me today. Let's go over your plan for the business trip we will make next week. Do you have the plan, schedule, and the activities for our stay in Germany?"

"I only brought the plan, is that OK?"

"Oh, did you forget to bring the rest of the documents for our trip? You know this is a big deal!"

"Yes, I forgot to bring the rest of the stuff with me today, I was rushing to leave the house this morning and so I left the schedule and list of activities in my home office. Sorry about this. Should I go and grab them right now?"

"Oh, dear, no, no, don't worry about it. It's no big deal. You can always send me a copy when you get home. I hope you like working from home, Cody. We want you to be comfortable and have your own schedule."

"Thank you, Nancy! Yes, I love working from home, it's been my one and only dream since I graduated from college to work remotely. I'll go ahead and send you the rest of the documents when I go home."

"Thank you, Cody! That's perfect. I know you did a great job and have faith in you. Also, don't worry if every once a while you mess something up; we all mess up sometimes."

"Hey, Baby! Did you get a chance to go grocery shopping? I am starving and really want to eat when I get home. Hope you bought that rotisserie chicken I love, honey boy!"

"Ouch! Looks like I didn't get a chance to go grocery shopping; too busy with work today. Can you get everything you need for dinner on your way home? Sorry, I didn't mean to disappoint."

"Urg... Was really looking forward to an easy dinner tonight, but yeah why not, I`ll do it."

"Sorry love! I`ll do better next time. My manager was too demanding today and I couldn't leave work to do the shopping. I even told her that I have plans for tonight but things are crazy over here. It made me feel bad asking you to do the shopping, but I hope you understand."

"Bad boss! Haha, just kidding. It's alright I`m heading home little earlier than usual anyways."

"I am useless and don't deserve your love, baby! So sorry, I wanted to do the shopping and impress you with my cooking skills but things didn't turn out too good."

"I don't love you because you cook for me sometimes or do chores like grocery shopping, I love you for being you. I love you for lots of other reasons that are legit, solid, and real. I might get mad at you from time to time, but will not stop loving you! Just clearing the air."

Things felt to be headed the right direction with Cody after our second session. He seemed to be a in a better mood and morale when I talked to him a couple of days after our session and Cody said he was contemplating therapy to help him deal with his childhood trauma. I was absolutely over the moon when I heard Cody was going to seek professional help and right there we both decided that we could discontinue our sessions as Cody was doing the right thing and was after the real treatment that he needed. Cody showed up at my office about three months after our last session and brought me a box of assorted chocolate which is the best gift anyone can give me. I thank God for letting me help Cody.

Cody's case closed.

Jason – The weak boy

"How did you find me? I don't actually have an Instagram account so I'm kind of curious to see where you saw my ad."

"I don't understand what you are asking me. It sounds strange. I just found you online!"

"Oh, I'm sorry if I didn't make myself clear. I was real surprised to see you find me given that you told me that you are only active in Instagram and do not have much contact outside of your family circle. I may be wrong too but just being curious. That's why I asked."

"I saw one of your clients had posted about you on his Instagram page and said that you helped him become a whole new person. I am a follower of his and trust him with what he posts so I looked for you online and found your number. Hope that is OK with you?"

Jason made me feel a bit uncomfortable with his demeanor. It's not that he did anything inappropriate, it's more like he had this intense look in his eyes which at times seemed a bit mean and wild. I was not comfortable with that look but I did my best to be professional and not let his mean way of looking at me, get to me and I believe I succeeded. I'm not sure what exactly was wrong with Jason, he seemed cold blooded and heartless and I just couldn't figure what would get him to express feelings or emotions for that matter. He had this really insensitive way of interacting with me and I think that's how he was with others as well, that was his character and I knew I had to see him past through that cold facial expression. God knows if I could have dropped him I would have but my consciousness did not allow me to nor did my professionalism.

"Well, let's talk about why you are here and how I can help you. Shall we? Would you like some coffee or tea? I like to make sure you feel comfortable here in my office so we connect great. The success of these sessions depend on how well the two of us connect."

"Coffee, black is fine, thanks!"

"Wow, you like black coffee with no milk or sugar? That, I think, means that you are a very serious young man. Am I right?"

"I don't know, it depends on how you define seriousness."

"Good answer. Here you go, be careful it's still really hot."

"Thank you, ma'am!"

"Ok, so tell me how I can help and what you are trying to get out of these sessions with me."

Jason, sipped his coffee and stared into space for a few seconds, then looked me in the eye and said, "I'm not sure how you can help me, but do what you did for your other clients."

"Hmm.... I work and help each one of my clients in a different way. Basically, I customize my sessions for each client and set an intention based on what my client needs are. So, I guess I really need to see what your needs are so I can proceed."

"As you can see I have never done this before and I'm not sure how these sessions flow. I mean I know what therapy is but I know this isn't therapy so I need you to tell me what you want from me. What do I say now? Where do I start? Or how do I start shall I say?"

"Why don't you tell me what you saw in your friend, you know... the one whom you follow on Instagram that made you want to reach out to me? Did he seem happier? Calmer? More successful? It's just that what we see in Instagram isn't always the truth. So tell me a bit more so I know whatever you saw in him really came from me."

"Haha... he posted a picture of him drinking a piña colada topless somewhere in South America on a nice beach with a nice dog and hot girlfriend. That's what I saw and I liked it. OK! Wait! He mentioned sometimes all you need is a little push to reach our pinnacle, the maximum capacity of our being, and that's what I want. I need a little push to do better."

"Is there anything about you that is holding you back from reaching your full potential?"

"Yes, me! I am holding myself back. I cannot connect with people the way most people connect. I mean, I try to act like others and say the same normal things they say but people just don't connect with me and try to avoid me. It makes me feel like I`m a weirdo! I don't think I say or do anything weird and sometimes I triple check the things I`m about to say just to make sure my words line up and are appropriate. Still, people don't like me, I guess!"

"Can you tell me about the latest situation you encountered such reaction from people?"

"Yeah, it was probably last week at company gathering. I was just trying to have fun and chit chat like anybody else while roaming around. People would talk to me for about a minute then went to find somebody else to talk to. It made me feel like I didn't belong there or wasn't wanted there. I don't like to feel bad for myself but I feel bad for me."

"The people who left after speaking to you for just a minute, did they find somebody else to talk to?"

"Definitely. Almost immediately they bumped into somebody else and talked to them."

"How long did they talk to the new person for?"

"Very long! Haha .... Very longer than they talked to me. I mean, other people just connect with each other, but they don't connect with me. I often wonder if I`m a freak or just different."

"OMG, nobody is a freak ... please do not use these terms to describe yourself, eventually they will get to you and you start believing them. It is extremely crucial that you don't belittle yourself. Now, we need to find out what is pushing people away from you. What is preventing people from connecting with you? Is it your general demeanor? It could be that people perceive certain demeanor of yours, as hostile or unfriendly. If I asked those people why they decided to end their conversation with you and move on and talk to somebody else, what do you think they would tell me?"

"Hmmm.... Let me think. This is probably a very good question to get to the bottom of my issues. Uh, I wanted to say I don't know why people leave after a minute of interaction with me but the truth is, if I thought hard enough about it, I would know: I come across as hostile and antisocial!"

"I see... so you think you come across as hostile an antisocial. How do you show your hostility? I'm pretty sure you have an idea because a lot of times we know what we are doing, but may not want to confront ourselves for various reasons."

"By making intense eye contact and keeping that eye contact for a long period of time without being sensitive to the other person's feelings. I know people see me as a hostile person."

"What about the antisocial label that you gave yourself? What do you do that would make people think you are antisocial?"

"I guess I don't display emotions. I mean it's not that I don't have emotions, it's just that I think most people display fake emotions and their facial expressions are just overly fake and inauthentic. But, I don't hate people, I may dislike them at times but I do want to have friends and go places with them. I like to be a part of a group or community or even a small team."

"I know what you mean. The fact that you want to be a part of a community shows you are not antisocial and don't have bad intentions in your relationships with people. I think you are not animated and are very frank and straight forward which at times, depending on the situation you are in, could be perceived as your disinterest in people. When talking to strangers, or coworkers, sometimes we have to be fake and say things we don't really mean, like complementing people on something they care about. It's hard, I know. I don't like doing it, and that is exactly why I left the corporate world and started my own business. I did not want to get invited to those exhausting Christmas parties or any kind of work gathering, even doing lunch with coworkers I was not close with was hell of a work. I realize these engagements are necessary and well, part of the corporate world. I highly recommend that if you don't like going to those gatherings, find a job that does not require you attending those parties. Now, in regards to people perceiving you as an antisocial, I think you need to try a bit harder and go out of your way, even when you don't like to, Its just what we do in our society and everybody has to be onboard with such ridiculous show. You know what I mean, right?

"Oh, God...I know, I know...but how do I force myself to be a clown in this show? I'm afraid I won't be able to keep up the faking for too long and then in the middle of the conversation I'll fall back on my default mode. Everybody is going to freak out if I go back to how I am and will avoid me at all cost. I mean, if I work really hard I'll be able to pretend that I'm interested in listening to the other person's story and show emotions and sync with their facial expressions, but once I get bored, I'm just going to do what I want to do: look as bored as one can be."

"You really do have a great personality, and I envy your future wife, Jason! I mean it. The woman who is going to become your future wife will have a great man by her side. You are authentic and real, and cannot tolerate fake people, that is a great quality in a man."

"Wow...I did not expect that! Thank you for complimenting me on my personality. To be honest, I never thought anybody would see my faulty personality as a good thing. It made me feel better, but I still have doubts my future wife would see my inability to fake things as a good thing. You know?"

"I get it. But, trust me, your future wife is one lucky woman. You'll see for yourself soon!"

"So, how are you going to help me with my strange personality? Can you help for real?"

"Here is the thing. I am a moral person and have strong work ethics, and just like how doctors will not order chemotherapy for a healthy person, I will not be doing sessions with you. Let me elaborate on that. You do not need my help at all! You are fully aware of what is causing your discomfort in your social interactions and the only reason you're not taking the right step is because you simply do not want to become something you don't enjoy being. Now, there are two ways you can address this issue: the first option is to accept the fact that not being a part of a larger group (community) is too painful and that you need it so bad that you have to learn to go with the system and become a fake dude, of course only in social settings. Then, the other option is to continue being awkward in company gatherings and not give a damn about what people think of you and don't mind not being liked by others. You can always build on your personal life and make it your best part of your life. I think the latter option is a smarter option.

"Wow, this must be the very first time somebody is telling me that I`m actually alright and do not need professional help. To be honest, what you just said made me really optimistic about myself and my future; I guess I`m not the freak I always imagined myself to be. I need to live my life and be myself, just knowing that I will not be turned down by people is a huge step in my entrance to the world. I always wanted to be accepted by others and have a community."

"What do you think your first step towards building your ideal life is going to be?"

"I think I`ll just relax into being me, how so every awkward I maybe. I want to be comfortable in my own skin so I`m just not going to care too much about what others say."

What's better than making your client's life better and what is more rewarding than hearing them feel better about themselves and being ashamed of who they are. I have done my part of the work, and although I did not make a whole lot of money out of these sessions, they inner satisfaction and happiness is through the roof. This is what I live for! My baby girl has been sleeping a lot today and it may be time to wake her up to go for our daily walk in my most favorite hiking trail. Having a dog is the kind of blessing you are thankful for everyday of your life and it's the kind of blessing not everybody gets to experience. I am forever thankful for my baby girl, I love her to death and the last day of her life will be the last day of my life.

Adam – It's always my fault

How can it all be Adam's fault when the world is so messed up? I was just working on a book and stupidly overwrote the latest version and replaced by the older version, is that my fault? Yes, it is. But if I made that mistake because somebody had got on my nerves arguing about something really stupid then it is their fault too, right? Well, we have to take responsibility for our mistakes and shortcoming and that goes for everyone. So, next time somebody distracts you and does not allow you to focus on what you actually need to focus on, let them know that if you mess something up or get called out at work for not performing the way you should, they need to apologies for their ill doing. But, that was not the case with Adam. He was always apologizing as if everything and anything that went wrong on this planet was purely his fault and that he had to beg for forgiveness no matter what. I remember when I met him the first time in a nice café in NYC, he looked at me with his beautiful eyes and said, "I`m sorry it's raining today." I actually started laughing hysterically out of blue and could not stop myself which was embarrassing, and told Adam it was so amazing that he would apologize for rain. I mean did he bring the rain? I love rain, if anything I should have thanked him for it and maybe rewarded him with some coffee or a tea at that café.

So, what was Adam like? Adam was young, kind of like most of my other clients, and he was also extremely shy and hard on himself. He reminded me of a colleague I had back in a day when I worked at an aerospace company where Brandon who sat right next to me made me feel like a toughie because he was always shy and insecure. Compared to Brandon I was very tough and thick skinned and never really came across as shy. Adam was also very quiet and would only talk when absolutely necessary or when he wanted to apologize for something he wasn't responsible for which made me feel bad for him. He was curious to see what my services offered and whether it could help him with his progression in life as an individual. I really like it when people show curiosity about what I do, I mean who doesn't like others to take interest in what they do and ask them questions and challenge them on how their career can improve. I always look for advice from both my clients and random people I talk to every once in a while. Adam asked how my services are any different from therapy or psychological helps people get from a certified professional. That was actually a really good question and something I was prepared to be asked.

"Well, I am not a certified therapist or medical personnel. My services provide a vision, a door to the other side of your world where the grass maybe greener, it maybe not greener or even browner. I don't know. Only you have to walk there to see for yourself if the grass is actually greener on the other side. If it is indeed greener on the other side, then you can start getting professional help and actually tackle whatever it is that's holding you back from achieving your full potentials. Most people do not take that first step towards being who they want to be, because they never get to see what it's like being that person. That happy person is such a stranger so distant from you that you cannot see it clearly. There is an idea of who that person is and how he looks, but not clear. My job is to show you who that person is and whether you want to live him, the way he lives inside you."

"Wow... that sounds terrific! You really do have an exciting and rewarding job, don't you?"

"I do! And now that I have it, I'll never go back to that soul sucking corporate job I dreaded so much."

"I am trying to leave coding too. I work at a startup and the owner is my best friend which is the reason I accepted that job at first place. Later I really regretted my decision. Too many work hour works and not a good pay or personal time off. I wish I could go back and told him "No!" but it's too late. I have been in this company for four years now and it has drained all my energy, really I got no energy or motivation left to pursue personal interests outside of work. Life is dull, too dull to live."

"Why don't you quite? I mean, you are an at will employee so you can leave whenever you like. Why waste your life away or better yet as most YouTubers like to put it "slave it away" when there is so much more to life than coding at a company that works you to death?"

"Trust me I have gone through all these thoughts and doubts. I cannot leave because I don't want to betray my best friend, I will lose him for sure to say the least. I don't want him to think I am not loyal to him."

"Can you tell me what happens if he thinks he is not loyal to you? I mean, worse comes to worst, you lose a friend who isn't even fair to you knowing how hard you work for him."

"I know, I know! I just need to get my shit together and then I'll be able to go my way and do what I want to do. I want to get angry at people a lot of times but instead I apologize to them to avoid conflict or even physical violence. I am always worried about getting confrontational with people."

"Confronting people does not have to be a negative thing if done correctly and with respect. I confront people who don't do their jobs right, and when I confront them I make sure to express my anger, not to lash out but to politely explain to them my frustration. There is nothing wrong with that in my world and I have never gotten in trouble for confronting wrong do-ers."

"I always envy people like you: strong, powerful, and determined. I feel bad for myself not to be able to stand up for myself and tell people to F*** off when they do something wrong. I mean when you don't confront them, they are further enabled to cause damage to others and I blame myself for it. I want help, and I like to know if you can help me see what's on the other side?"

"Of course, Adam! I can help you see for yourself what it's like to be what you want to be."

Adam was a sweet young man who wanted to live his full potential and progress as a human being. He was done taking the back seat and was ready to be in the driver seat and take control of the world around him. After our meeting, I went home and made a nice lunch for my baby girl who was sleeping on the sofa like an angle. She always gave me this fuzzy feeling that I cannot describe to people who don't know what true bonding is. It's Oxytocin that controls this great fuzzy feeling and I wish everybody could experience it to see how beautiful and comforting bonding with another live being can be. I do believe that some people are actually unable to bond because their oxytocin levels are pretty low and therefore they never get to experience what the rest of us experience. Suddenly, Adam came to my mind. Did he know what it feels to truly bond and become one with another being; almost as if your existence depends on the other being. When I opened the door my baby girl woke up from her beauty nap and was so warm and cute. I hugged her and pet her head and back, so adorable my baby girl is. Then, when my baby girl had enough cuddling, I went to the kitchen and made some coffee and fed my baby girl a nice warm lunch. I sat down on the sofa and watched her eat, all the noise she was making when eating her favorite meal (steak) was so appealing to me. Was Adam capable of feeling love? Of course, he was. What a silly question to ask, Adam was a normal man who wanted to love and be loved, who doesn't want that? I started thinking about what I needed to do for Adam and the plan I had to put together to see what best helps him get over his anxiety over interacting with people and not just strangers but his friends too. The first thing I had to consider was: what makes people avoid difficult and complex interactions with others? For example, confrontation. What makes people steer clear of confronting people who do them wrong? Fear of being conceived as trouble maker or maybe unlikeable. That is scary for someone with low self-esteem, I understand. In this world you have to have a thick skin to be able to face the hardships and hurdles life throws at you. Now, what's the benefit of confronting people? You hold on to your core values and make yourself believe you are appropriate to life as you are. You become proud of yourself and stand up for yourself which further builds self-confidence and self-respect. With confidence you can live your best life, without it you only endure life and stand it for as long as you can, then give up and leave this planet without having ever lived your best life.

That's what Adam needed: self-esteem and confidence in himself. I immediately started working on a good scenario that could make Adam see what self-confidence could do for him and if you ask me, I say I put together a pretty smart scenario. I focused on the scenario to give him exactly what he needed and nothing else. I worked straight without distraction for two hours and then got up to take a little walk outside since my baby girl needed her daily dose of vitamin D as well. When I walked out the door a cool breeze felt my face and right then I realized that autumn had arrived with all its pretty colors. I looked at my baby girl and noticed she was sniffing the air and I guess she was noticing Miss Autumn too. She started wagging her tail and moving her butt side to side showing contentment and happiness: how perfect was that moment? Even though I don't believe in God, I thank God every day for my life and the quality of life I have. I know lots of people do not have the quality of life that I have and I feel for them, however, I think people get used to the poor quality of their living situation and overtime see that as normal life.

"Adam, thanks for coming in today so we can discuss my plan for you. Would you like to have some coffee first?"

"Sure thing, I actually need some caffeine in me before we start. I didn't sleep too well last night; my neighbors are so noisy and it disrupts my sleep. I have tried to be nice to them and that didn't work, they just do what they please."

"Why not call the police on them? Don't you think they need to face the consequences of their disrespectful behavior?"

"Well, I'm the nice guy who tries to be patient with people and also understanding so what can I say? This is me."

"Maybe, time to change? I mean do you want to take a peak and what's on the other side? Maybe, you'll like it."

"Sure, I think I'm already sick of being who I am and losing to mean people over and over again because I cannot stand up for myself and stick to my guns. I need to respect my own wants, they are legit and I am not asking for too much. I need to be taken seriously and treated fairly by people and that is not the case right now because I'm too soft with bad asses."

"Hi, Adam... I am your neighbor, and noticed you parked in my spot. Can you please move your car so I can park?"

"Well, nice to meet you neighbor and good to know you have been enjoying parking in my spot long enough that you thought it's your parking spot. This is my parking spot and it's OK that you have been using it, but I would like to have it back so please stop parking at my spot and talk to property management to see where you can park your car. OK?"

"Hah! For real? I mean, this has been the spot where I parked, so what changed? Why can't I park here anymore?"

"It's just that it's been my parking spot and I allowed you to park for a while but now it's time to get it back. Please talk to the property management as I said because I don't actually owe you any explanation."

"Wow, how rude. Aren't you one of those lonely men who can't get women and so they become the enemy of women?"

"Say, what you want to say. And, reach out to the property management to get information on your parking spot."

"How did this feel? Did you feel like you were going to pass out or something? Did it make you too uncomfortable?"

"Actually, it felt like an out of body experience, I never talked to anyone like that, and it made me feel bad about myself."

"It's because you stood up for yourself and by standing for yourself you announced to the world that you deserve respect. You claimed your fair share of existence and let that person know that you are a worthy person and will stick to your guns."

"Well.... I am not sure about doing this in real life and feeling OK about it. It's more like a traumatizing experience."

"You won't feel OK about right away. I don't want you to get the wrong idea, these exercises take time, and you need to allow time to fix things for you. You need to exert yourself and be assertive with your wants. You exist and people need to acknowledge your rights, otherwise you will confront them and make them respect you. It takes time for you to build self-esteem and you are most definitely going to feel the pain of growth which is normal and should not discourage you from bettering yourself. I know this is going to help you. Let's continue these sessions and let's do more of a real life thing maybe in public so you can get used to asserting yourself where there are others watching you."

"What you are saying makes sense to me, and I`m still too scared and frozen from the session we just did. I`m worried."

"Everything you are worried about are legit, and I get that you don't want to be confrontational, but I think this is the best course of treatment you can receive to bring out the new you. Your new versions is going to be a much happier person and you will have a much full filling life. Think about it. Take the pain now, and have a much better life later. Will you do it?"

After five more sessions, Adam finally became comfortable in my sessions and we took our working sessions to public and got quite a stare and attention from strangers. People sometimes tried to interfere, not knowing the conflicts Adam and I had were staged, and Adam eventually got used to being stared at. He also became comfortable with claiming his rights and sticking to his guns, something he previously would be traumatized of. I did put Adam through hell, but the outcome was unbelievable. Adam became a new man who knew how to defend himself and not give in just because somebody told him to back off.

I was proud of myself. I had helped someone make a lifelong change and I needed to celebrate. There is only one way I celebrate my accomplishments: a large chocolate cake and fast food. That's what I did that weekend and suddenly life became a lot brighter than before. I guess it's the power of helping people that shines light into your life and it's priceless.

Robert – The empty shell

How do I describe Robert? He was a fifty plus year old white man, dressed like a 50 something year old white man, acted like an old dude and was sad like an old man. He had worked all his life in Construction and was now a project manager. I don't know if I mentioned, but I did work in Construction for a few years and I absolutely hated it. I hated the people (most people) who I worked with and interacted with on daily basis, they were mostly people with criminal background and that's the kind of people Construction desires so those people can be worked to death. It was pretty sad to witness the abuse construction workers had to endure in order to be employed. I left Construction as soon as it was no longer worth the money and thank God I have a bachelor's degree and was able to land another job in a high-tech almost as soon as I decided to leave Construction. Anyway, that was some context for you to know where Robert came from and how he was treated all his life.

Robert was basically an empty shell, that's the best and most accurate way to put it. Yes, he was desperately looking to fill himself with something, an idea, ideology, something that he could own and regard as his solid red pill. Robert was not my favorite person, but he was my client, and I always give my best to my clients no matter who they are and what their background is.

I knew what I needed to do and had a clear idea of what was going to work for Robert, he was going to be an easy breezy project for me.

"Robert, we discussed your situation the other day and I am happy to tell you that your case is probably the smoothest case for me. There are many like you. Middle aged men who have been worked like machines all their life and provided for their family just to reach 50 and suddenly realize they've lived all these years and got nothing to show for it."

"Well, I was actually hoping to be a bit more than just a 50-year-old man who has nothing to his name."

"You are more than that! Of course, you are. My point is this is how older men see themselves: an old being with no worth."

"aha"

"So, I do have a plan for you and am hoping to start our first session pretty soon, maybe this upcoming Monday?"

"Sure, that works!"

"I'll send you the plan so you can read through the script and come prepared to our session. If you don't have time to read your script ahead of time, that's fine too, we'll get you up to speed when you get here."

"Sounds good, I won't have time to read the script until I get here anyway. So much work to do. I work in an industry that works you to death which is cruel, and I know that. I wish I could leave this slavery and become somewhat my own person and figure out what it is I want to do with my life, or with myself. I am already 50 and don't have a whole lot of time left. You see, my health has been in decline and having worked in such a harsh industry, which is physically extremely demanding, has left me with awful health. I am not going to make it to 65, I know it and it makes me anxious, sometimes hopeless. I want help but I don't know how you can help. Last night I was thinking about these sessions, and it occurred to me that I am just wasting money and that nothing useful is going to come out of these sessions with you. I feel stuck! Yes, but do I want to waste money on something that may or may not work? If you were in my shoes, what would you do?"

"Thank you for being up front and telling me how you really feel about my services and how I am going to help you. I mean it. A lot of people wait for too long before they ask these questions. Here is what I tell you, I do believe these sessions will help you see yourself as a happy person. You'll see what it's like to be on the other side and be content with yourself and your life without worrying about not living your best life. A lot of people have come here, sat on the exact chair you are sitting on and voiced the exact same concern that you voiced. A lot of people think these sessions are just a waste of money, just like you said, and that I am basically, scamming them. Yes, some people think I am exploiting their loneliness and making money off their misery. Well, this is not exploitation and what about the psychologists who make a ton of money off mentally ill? I am helping people and have good intentions. What do you think about what I just said?"

"Well, I must say I am a man of few words, like most men, but I do have to say that you convinced me to at least do the first session with you and see how it goes. I mean, you really seem like a lovely person, and I do enjoy your company, it's just that with all the scams going on all over the world, trusting a new person is a scary thing."

"Absolutely! I understand you 100%. But look, you know my office address and every information you need to track me down should I scam you, right? So, you really got nothing to worry about and I want to make sure I address all your concerns before proceeding."

"I think we are good to proceed at this point. Like I said, I really like you and I want to see where this journey will take me. At this point, ha-ha, it's funny, I don't have a whole lot to lose anymore. I mean I have my family, but, they are selfish too! They have used me all these years and made me work like an animal to a breaking point so they could have what they wanted. It's a shame that I don't even like my own family and I cannot tell anyone but you this. I feel like I have been used and exploited all these years, all these lonely years, and I did the best I could. No more sacrificing! I am done. So, let's do this and hopefully this will be a turning point for me. I want my experience in these sessions to take me down to the bottom of the ocean, and then I'll decide once and for all whether I find enough value in life to come back up to the surface, to break the surface and have a breakthrough in life. So, let's do this!"

"Robert, I am so moved by you. I'm so sorry to hear about your family using you to get what they wanted in life, but you do not have to put up with that. You know if you don't end up liking my sessions, you should still make a change and turn your life around. You deserve much more and from the bottom of my heart I am sorry to hear all this. How about I give you my first session for free?"

"It's Ok, love! I know you need to make ends meet and I don't want you to suffer because you are trying to gain my trust. I already trust you!"

Robert wasn't my favorite person up until that conversation. Wow, I did judge that poor man! I did! I am guilty of judging my client who came here asking for my help in despair and I was not as kind as I should have been to him. Why? Why did I feel differently about him inside? Looks like I had best dig deep and see what's going on inside of me. Does Robert remind me of somebody who I made me dirty in the past? Who does Robert remind me of? Maybe, my own father. Yeah, that's it, Robert reminds me of my dead-beat father who was only a great inconvenience to all of us when we all lived together. He was always angry, always agitated by every little thing we did. I hated seeing him coming home from work. I wanted a truck to run him over. One time I remember we were driving with him in the car when a truck approached us on the other side of the road and almost ran us over. I wanted so badly for my dad to die but did not want my siblings and I to get hurt. We did not deserve to get hurt but my dad did. Unfortunately, the truck did not hit us, and life went on just as it was going before. I am glad those days are over, but for the first time in a very long time I thought of my dad, and it might mean that I need to seek therapy to see how to deal with my childhood pain and scars. I know a lot of therapists who go to therapy for themselves and there is no shame in doing that. You always need help, no matter who you are and what you do for a living. I'll call Andrew (my bestie) to see if he knows of a good therapist who can see me as soon as possible. I don't want to do these sessions with Robert when I have such harsh feelings about my own dad. Poor Robert reminded me of my dad and it's not Robert' fault.

The thought of going to therapy was sort of relieving, it was almost as if a heavy load had been lifted from my shoulders. I knew I needed help for a long time, just didn't have a good enough reason to actually seek help. That was enough for that day and so I got up, took a long hot shower, treated myself to some sweets, journaled a bit, cooked, then went to bed. That day I went to bed early because my brain was tired of thinking excessively about my childhood trauma and the sadness and helplessness I experienced then. I carried all that pain throughout my life and maybe now it was time to put that load down, like what Robert was doing for himself. Wow, I was actually learning from Robert. That night I slept with some anxiety, and I was aware of it, just as much as my body was aware of the consequences of anxiety. I needed Andrew's help so I could move this hurdle out of the way, I knew I had to go to therapy.

The next morning, I was feeling much better and of course it was a new day. I thank God or universe for these new days. What if days never renewed and just continued on and on and on. We would all be depressed out of our mind if the days did not renew. I took a quick shower that morning, then went about my morning routine. I peeked out the window and noticed it had rained earlier and the ground was all wet. I love rain and I know the rainy days are mine, and only mine. That day was going to be a great day for me, there was no way that day would have been ruined by anything, it was my day! I checked my phone and saw there was a message from Robert saying he was feeling really good about our upcoming session and that he was glad we had that conversation the other day. I knew that day was my day. The rain always brings me the best. I responded to Robert saying that I too was so happy that we talked and cleared the air and that our next session was going to be awesome!

My dog was sitting in front of the kitchen glass door looking at rain so curiously that the cuteness almost killed me. My baby girl murders me when she is just being her, doing nothing of significance; that's her superpower. My mind was occupied with my dog, and I did not want to go and do anything else, knowing that I needed to start writing a scenario for Robert I got up and stood behind my work desk and started putting together a scenario for Robert's next session.

"Robert, why don't you join us for some drinks this weekend? We are going to Pap's bar down the street."

"Thanks for the invite, friend! I got a few things I've got to take care of this weekend so I won't be able to join this weekend."

"What?!?! That is unlike you! Since when you reject our invite and don't hang out with your old buddies."

"Since today! Is that going to be a problem for you Tony?"

"It is not going to be a problem, man! Just wondering, though, why you don't want to go with us to get some drinks."

"Didn't you hear my answer?"

"Man oh man! You sure have changed. Without us you've got nothing going on. I mean if we don't hang out with you, you have nothing else going on. You need us so you have something in your life. I mean other than your mean family."

"Hah, never looked at our friendship that way. And, even if I don't have anything else in life, I wouldn't want somebody who talks me down to be my friend, no matter how empty my life is. You do not talk to your friends like that, it's that simple. And, just so you know, I am my own person and have things to do, things that I enjoy doing, and hubbies to keep me occupied."

"Well, without us you do not have a community to support you. Who is going to have your back if not us?"

"You are too funny now, man! When did you or the other guys ever have my back? Maybe, I have become forgetful but I just don't think I remember a time when you helped me with anything at all. So, it's kind of easy for me to let go of our so called friendship and focus on my own hubbies and activities that actually bring me joy. Have fun drinking, I guess."

"So, how did you feel about this first session? Do you see where you can improve the image you have of yourself?"

"This was embarrassing to me. I don't want to be the one who stands alone and acts like they are worthy even when their group of friends no longer want them. I have never been this person and just playing that scenario bothered me greatly."

"It's normal. You are supposed to be bothered that's foreign to you because your mind immediately registers that sort of talk as a threat to who you currently are. Your mind always wants to be in its default mode because that is its safety blanket."

"Do you think I should continue these sessions?"

"It's all up to you. If you are asking if I think you can improve with these sessions, the answer is absolutely. Don't feel bad about that embarrassment you felt, it's part of the change process we are introducing to your mind. Your mind will play games and will trick you into believing that your existence is in danger, while it's not. We are just trying to inject some self-love and self-esteem to you and your mind is rejecting it, is exactly what I expected. I want you to know that gaining self-esteem so you are no longer an empty shell, is painful at first because it is going to shift your mindset and you have to be able to commit to these working sessions and maybe later on, if you are comfortable, therapy. It all comes down to you."

"I like to think about it a bit more when I got home to make sure it's the right thing for me to do."

"Sounds absolutely fair and reasonable. Please feel free to call me or text me, if you are more comfortable with texting, in case you have concerns or questions."

Robert completed twenty sessions and we still have a little more work to do before we can say that Robert has built self-esteem and is finally able to do what pleases him without worrying about what others think of him. Out of all my clients, Robert was the most broken one and I felt so sorry for him. His family was not the nicest and definitely could have supported him throughout this process more. Robert was an example of a man who had a family but felt very much lonely and no real friends to cheer him up. Every in his life was built around societal pressure and the things the society valued, not what he valued as a person and that was depressing Robert. Slowly, with my sessions, he felt more comfortable accepting himself as he was, and not minding how others perceived him which was life altering for him.

Now, moving on to the next client of mine. I feel so much more fulfilled working for myself and seeing the result of the effort and sacrifice I make compared to the corporate job I had a while ago. I am so lucky to be able to work for myself and have my own schedule. My baby girl has been thriving with me being home most of the time and this means I am living my very best life.

Jordan – Everybody stinks

My Jordan was a good-looking young man, the kind you wish you could have in your life either as a boyfriend, husband, or son. He was just a sweet young man, and I loved him since I laid eyes on him. Softspoken, shy, quiet but kind and generous. Jordan had other characteristics as well that were just as lovely and all in all he was a nice young man. I never expected him to tell me that he hated everybody and anybody whom he came into contact with. Unbelievable! Jordan was too sweet to hate anybody, and I was adamant about not believing that.

"Love changes everything! It makes everything colorful and pretty, it makes life enjoyable and meaningful. Without love, life is aimless, too harsh to bear, too long to endure, so why live it. Of course, if you never had love in your love, you`ll never know what it feels to be in love, so you live your life aimlessly and eventually die. But, for me, I am done with life."

"What do you want from me, Jordan?"

"I know the kind of service you offer and provide to your clients. I wanted to meet up with you to see if there is anything you can do for me."

"I can definitely provide you with the kind of service you need the most. Jordan, you need to see life as is not how you want it to be."

"How do I want life to be? What do I want from this life filled with suffering and misery?"

"I don't believe you want to suffer like this which is why you are kicking and screaming, pushing people away, being bitter, and not wanting your family around you."

"Nah, I don't like my family and got no friends to worry about."

"Jordan, you are so generous, let's see why you are not sharing the love in your heart with those around you."

"I sort of don't care to share the love I have in my heart with others. What's the use of it anyway?"

"Then, what is it that I can do for you?"

"I want to be able to love again. I want to be loved and feel like I'm somebody's highest priority and not just a dude who needs to provide for somebody else. Even my family thinks I should provide for them when they are very much capable of taking care of themselves. They see me as an ATM which they can draw money from when they want and if they don't get their way, they don't want to talk to me."

"What you are describing here is brutal. No one is to carry that weight on their shoulders. You deserve respect and love from your family and friends."

"Since I'm not getting that from them and my ex, I think I am doomed to be alone forever. But I don't want to die like this, I want to die knowing that I am loved and desired."

"Well said! So, now let's see what I can do for you. Shall we?"

"I am excited to hear."

"You need to see that you are not your money. You are not just an ATM machine which people come to take money from, and you are a human being with deep feelings and emotions. It doesn't matter if people don't see that in you, what really matters is that you see it for yourself and start valuing your authenticity. Self-worth comes from self-esteem."

"You've got a plan for me to gain self-esteem?"

"You bet! Let me put that plan together and we can meet again early next week to discuss what I have put together for you. Then we are going to work on you. Just remember, things don't happen overnight. It takes time and it takes effort for you to get to the other side. Let's be patient with the process."

"Deal!"

After Jordan left, I was left baffled and maybe a little bit angry with him, why would such a good-looking young man who had his whole life ahead of him allow himself to fill his tank with anguish and hatred toward himself? Ok, so his family did not have his back and did not treat him right, but Jordan seemed much wiser than that; he knew his family wasn't a nurturing one and so why doubt your self-worth? And then inside I felt this fire burning my inside; anger that turned into rage has always been my number one enemy. I was no longer too young and inexperienced, not knowing what I needed to do to make myself feel better. Fidgeting is the solution to most my anger issues, I always need to move, get up, walk around, stroll around the building, clean up the kitchen, vacuum and as long as I have something to do, I'm all good. I knew my bathroom needed some deep cleaning, so I pulled up my sleeves and got to work.

For the new few days, I put my head down and poured all my energy and focus into making an exceptional action plan for my Jordan. I basically locked myself in my apartment and lived off black coffee to finish up the plan as promised to Jordan.

"Hi, Jordan... how are you doing?"

"Hi, yeah, not too bad, I guess... I went out and got some Vitamin D which was very much needed. So, feeling good."

"Oh, good for ya! I need to go out and get my fair share of Vitamin D. I called you to let you know that I have put together your plan and was wondering if this upcoming Monay at 11 in the morning would work for you to meet up?"

"Monday? Well, let me see my plans for Monday.... Yeah, yeah, looks like I can make it at 11 in the morning. Would it take longer than an hour?"

"I think an hour is enough. See you on Monday."

Jordan sounded insecure and somewhat gloomy over the phone. He wasn't excited about our upcoming meeting and even when I told him that I had put together his action plan he didn't sound interested. I had a feeling Jordan was going to cancel our Monday meeting, and that is exactly what happened.

Monday morning rolled and I got a text message from Jordan saying he wasn't feeling too well that morning and that he wanted to cancel our session. I told him not to worry about it and that we could always meet another time. My gut feeling was telling me Jordan was having second thoughts about having these sessions with me and so I decided to get a little creative. I texted Jordan the next day asking how he was feeling. He responded saying he wasn't at his best but doing better than yesterday. I asked if he wanted to meet up for a fun activity, like rock climbing or going to a cat café, something that would interest him. I told him it was an open invitation and that if he wasn't interested it was Ok; the goal was to connect in a deeper level so I could better help him. He responded saying although he liked the idea, his workload was excruciating and that he wouldn't be able to make time for our fun activity. I kind of expected that response and he sounded genuine and respectful.

Days were starting to go gray with fall approaching and I must admit, fall has always been my favorite season and it's when my energy is the highest. I love cold and chilly weather, and my birthday is also in the middle of autumn which makes my love for the colorful season that much more special. Fridays are usually light for me, and I keep it that way to give my mind to rest and rejuvenate for the upcoming week. Jordan called me the Friday of the week we cancelled our Monday session and told me he was getting a cold foot and that he wasn't sure whether my services could actually give him what he wanted. He said faking happiness and staging a life he would be most happy with would only give him temporary satisfaction and wasn't enough to make him carry on with his life. He was looking for something solid, a solution that would transform him inside out, not just a few sessions of happiness. I was too familiar with that mindset, and I knew how to respond to him. I told him he was right and that everything we did was going to give him temporary contentment (if anything at all) with himself and his life and that it would soon be over once he got back to normal life. I said fake happiness wouldn't even last an hour after our session. The goal of these sessions, however, was not to give him something that would last longer than an hour or so, the goal was to show him what he was missing. He needed to decide for himself whether the greener grass on the other side was worth changing habits he was clinging to and whether the pain of change could be endured.

Jordan was convinced our sessions were worth giving a try and so the next Tuesday we set off to our first session.

"So, Jordan, I want you to trust me and know that we are going to accomplish something amazing here that'll transform your life. I have put together a plan of action for our sessions. You just have to play your role as written in these plans. I am going to hand over your sections. Here you go. Did you have any questions for me?"

"No, it's all clear. Let's do this."

"Hi… I saw you shopping at the grocery store the other day, I actually go there a lot. I wanted to say hi. I'm Liz."

"Hi, Liz… Nice to meet you! I'm Jordan."

"Hey, Can I invite you to dinner this weekend? I am really interested in getting to know you a bit more so it would be really nice if you accepted my invite."

"Uh, let me look at my schedule for this weekend."

"OMG, you usually have a schedule for your weekends?"

"No, but I have to make sure I don't have any other plans for this upcoming weekend. You know I have a lot of friends around here and we usually meet up for a drink or something. I am more into nature, so I go hiking with them too and we have a lot of fun in the forest."

"Listen, I cannot do this! This is bizarre! I don't need to lie like this. I have no friends and I do not do anything over the weekends, just sit at home and watch something on YouTube so why should I sit here and lie?"

"Jordan, we are staging this to show you what your life could be like and if you participate and lose yourself in this play, you'll see what you are missing. Its ok if you don't want to have lots of friends and that you don't do anything on your weekends, but the goal here is that you see how it feels to have all this."

"Alright, lets continue with this game."

"Ok, so let me give you my number so you can text me and let me know."

"Sounds good! Bye, Liz. Nice meeting you!"

"Good job, Jordan. I know this meant nothing to you, but we are going to continue until you really melt into your role, then you`ll taste what you have been missing. Then, you decide if you are willing to seek psychological help and therapy to become who you want to become."

"It was painful to be someone who I envied for so long. It pains me to think there are people out there who are approached by girls asking them out. I have always been on the corner, in the shade and nobody even noticed me."

"The pain is the growing pain. You`ll get there. I`ll see you in our next session."

Jordan baffled me big time, his demeanor screamed "confident", but deep down he was incredibly unconfident. I was mostly worried about his perception about the world we live in; everything was all or nothing to him and that is a detrimental mindset. I believed Jordan when he said that he hated people around him and basically disliked people in general. When you look at the world from his unrealistic lens, you tend to have this distorted view of the intentions behind people's actions. He had trust issues, serious trust issues and that was going to be a problem for us working together, what is a help if there is no trust in it? I had serious work ahead of me and the first step was to gain Jordan's trust and I knew how to do that.

"Jordan, I just called to see how you are doing. You don't have to call me back, just checking on you and making sure you are ready for our second session. The next session is going to be different, I like to discuss with you the other cases I worked on before you and how I help those clients get their life back together. I know I should have done this in our first session or even before that but hope it's not too late. So, I guess I'll see you in our next session. Take care!"

After leaving Jordan that voicemail my nerves calmed down a bit. I jumped in the shower and took a quick shower before heading to the post office to return the summer dress I bought weeks ago for my upcoming vacation in Italy and the dress was just not to my liking so it was going back. I knew thunderstorms were coming that evening so I made sure to take care of everything before the weather turned wild. Around 8 in the evening, the thunderstorm started hitting us like hell and the rain started coming down which was pleasant since I like rain. Rain makes me feel comfortable in this uncomfortable world we live in, it lets me know that I'm still here and that Mother Nature has my back.

When I got home, I saw I had a text message from Jordan which made me feel so much better knowing he is OK. He basically said that he was doing well and that he had been struggling with inner demons trying to shut down negative self-talks and that he succeeded in getting himself together. I knew he could do it, he was a very strong young man and deserved love. We texted back and forth a few times and finally decided to meet up before our second session so we could talk about my past experiences with clients with similar background as him. Jordan liked that idea and was curious to see how he could resonate with the other clients.

Jordan was not necessarily a difficult person to deal with, he was simply too easy to understand and work with. We had a few sessions and after that Jordan decided that he could walk the rest of the recovery path by himself and no longer needed my help. I agreed and we parted ways.

I was happy for Jordan and happy for me. I was making good money and soon would be going to move to a townhome which looked more like a home than an apartment. I was making progress in life and was also building wealth. What more could I ask for.

Dave – Work and death, and nothing in between

I was strolling around my block with my dog, taking a bit of a break from work and hectic life while not being sure if walking in that heat was a good idea, when I came back to my normal busy life by my email notification. Looks like I had another client! One more angle on earth who needed my help to feel better about life. One more victim brought into this world to give purpose to parents who may or may not have had the means to raise a self-loving individual. We are all the same, but some of us who I guess we can call the lucky ones have figured out how to ignore the bullies. Now when I say bullies, don't assume I`m talking about the people who walk left and right looking for low confidence beings who cannot defend themselves. I`m not talking about them, I`m talking about regular boring life that forces you to survive and have your guard up all the time. Worst of all you must figure out how to make a living, hustle, manage a family, deal with inflation, and much more while being positive and looking enthusiastic about your future. That is how life bullies you, and nobody is immune from it, but you can learn to ignore it and manage it to a point where it is no longer your biggest enemy. I mean who am I kidding, you are never immune from life bullying, and everybody must carry their own fair share of misery.

My dog started barking at this little squirrel desperately trying to reach something that looked like a hazelnut but I`m not sure. I tried to pull back my dog by gripping hard on to her leash, but she was head over hills determined to get friendly with her new buddy. Though it was hot that day, the weather forecast had it that it was going to rain in the afternoon and so I must say I was in a good mood. I have always loved rain, ever since I can remember, rain brought joy and peace to my heart. My dog, however, fears rain for some reason and never actually liked it much.

I must not check my phone, my time with my dog and walking her around the block is always my doggy and me time for us and it is not to be disturbed by an email notification. I keep walking my dog trying to live the moment with my baby and free my soul from things that trouble me. Lately my clients have been getting more and more desperate and needy, and it hurts my heart to see so many people stuck in life unable to get out of the hole they have been digging for themselves for so long. They don't like themselves; they can only stand their own presence for a few minutes and then get irritated and start attacking others around them. Some don't even have anybody around them for distraction and so they self-harm. I take a deep deep breath, inhale and exhale as I was taught by Lucy, my yoga instructor, and try to calm my soul. It's all about wrapping yourself in positive and light energy then allowing your soul to submerge in its authentic self to feel itself and to be comfortable in its own skin. OK, now, don't ask me what all this means because I don't really know; these are the lessons taught by Lucy so ask her.

My dog kept pulling me in different directions, she is uneasy today, maybe she sensed rain is coming and that is making her anxious. Time to go home, I guess.

Taking a cold shower after walking in the heat is the best part of my day, it is in fact the highlight of my day. And of course, the love of my life, my dog, goes straight to her bed and cuddles up her stuffed animals like a cute toddler. I stand there, watching her do nothing and just exist, and I must hold back my tears: how beautiful can a being be? She is lovely, vibrant, full of life, and curious. What more could you ask for in life? Dogs are the solution to everything; they show the ultimate love and companionship. If you don't have one, go ahead and adopt one, they'll transform your life.

Cold water with lots of ice is a must, if I had some fruit juice or even coconut water, I would drink that to cool off. I feel much healthier after my walk and livelier having spent quality time with my fluffy buddy.

After an hour of break, I checked my phone to see what that email notification was all about. As I had expected, it was a new client asking about the service I offer. I responded back to him and let him know that I usually start the process by scheduling a ten-minute Zoom call to get to know the person I'll be working with and that if he was interested, we could probably meet the next day to discuss this further. I could tell from this potential client's tone that he was emotionally extremely congested and that he didn't have anybody to confine himself to. I had a lot of these clients, emotionally congested and extremely needy people who had hit rock bottom and had no idea where to go next. Most of these people had gone through therapy and while therapy is an effective way of facing your issues and it offers ways to deal with personal and psychological problems, they did not get what they were looking for in those therapy sessions. I do believe therapy and professional mental help is what they absolutely need, but if they don't want to take that route and instead inquire my service, I'll give it to them. I mean after all, that is how I make a living. Some call me a scam, a fraud, manipulator, exploiter, a woman who takes advantage of other's misery and makes money off stranger's inner demons eating them alive. I get all of that. But they are not forced to use my service, and they can absolutely do the right thing and head to therapy instead of using me to make them feel better. They come to me willingly and eagerly, they are not forced into this.

The next day I had my ten-minute Zoom call with Dave and got a feel for how his demeaner and personality were and from there I figured how I could serve him best. Dave said exactly what almost every other client of mine told me: I feel empty. Emptiness is probably the mother of all evils, well, most probably after fear. I assured him that he didn't have to worry about what was going on with him and that a lot of people had that emptiness, it's just that everyone find their own little way of dealing with it, some people overwork themselves almost to death, some turn to cult or religion (I use cult and religion interchangeably for obvious reasons), and some actually seek help.

Dave wanted to get to know me, and I guess he had every right to worry about how our session were going to go and how I was actually going to make him feel better. I went ahead and explained to him how I was going to work with him and he was going to use my services to see how the other side of misery (happiness) felt like. That's the thing with my clients, they have this illusion of happiness, this fantasy thought that life is better on the other side and that if they were on the other side, their life would have been perfect, now whatever perfect means to them. It may not be their life that is so bad, it may be their perspective and inability to see reality for what it really is. Delusion and illusion are the enemies of these men and Dave was no different.

Dave and I agreed on the service that I was going to provide to him, and we also discussed my fees and basically agreed on the terms and conditions of our work together. We then scheduled the meeting times when I was going to work with him and make him feel good.

The first day of our work together was scheduled for the upcoming Friday, after Dave finished work. Dave worked as a product manager for a High-tech company that focused on autonomous driving vehicles and was workaholic. He worked on average 80 hours a week and twice last year he fainted out of exhaustion in his bathroom at home. He did not seek medical help, let alone psychiatric help for his struggles and always blamed his workaholism on having too much work and responsibility at his company. His wife was completely estranged from him, and I don't blame her for it, I would have checked out emotionally from a man like Dave if I were married to him. The only thing that kept his wife, Elli, around was the finances and their three children who were all under 10. Elli wanted nothing to do with Dave, she basically lived a separate life from him and only needed his paycheck to pay the bills and kids' expenses. Again, I don't blame Elli for that. At first, I thought Dave suffered greatly from depression but after talking to him a bit more I realized there were lots of other issues going on with him, and depression was just a cherry on top.

Dave was raised by an aggressive and violent father who seemed to have hated Dave since he was born. And a mother who was always a victim or so she depicted herself as. Growing up life was awful for Dave, nothing and everything he did never made his father happy. He got a lot of beating from his angry father and never forgave him for it. He moved out by 18 when he got into university and never returned home, not even for Christmas or Thanksgiving. His mother did not bother calling him or texting him asking where he was or what he was doing in his life. It seemed like he lived in complete darkness all his life. He worked hard and got a job at a great High-Tech company and as he put it, it saved his life for a while. After marrying Elli, he thought he had his life together and that he was out of the darkness, nevertheless, all that darkness was now inside of him, and he no longer could escape the darkness as he was carrying it with him. The new phases of life, like the birth of his children, did not change the fact that he was miserable inside and wanted to feel happy. He wanted to know what it's like to be happy and when people seemed happy, he would try to put himself in their shoes to see what happiness really was but never actually felt that joy.

Last year, after having those two fainting episodes and his wife threatening him with divorce, he attempted to take his life and that of course failed. He then, found out about me from a coworker who was a client of mine, and decided to take a stab at seeking help from me.

"So, Dave I didn't know what you like to have with your coffee or tea so I brought in some chocolate muffins, but if there is anything else I can get you please let me know. I want you to be comfortable here."

"Oh, muffins are perfectly Ok."

"Ok, good! I wanted to go ahead and start our session by you telling me about what you hope to get out of our sessions together."

"I like to feel like others. I like to be somebody and feel like I'm somebody and enjoy that. I want to submerge myself in something other than just abstract thoughts, I want to feel. I want to feel life and experience what its like to just feel, and not think or wonder. I need your help to feel the kind of joy others feel when they are happy or fully content in the moment. I never actually let myself go, I never let myself use my senses, I always put myself down when I tried to feel the moment something as small as feeling rain on my skin, it was a no, no! I cannot continue like this; I don't want to die like this. I need to know that I lived a little and that I know what living outside of my head feels like. I want to laugh."

"This doesn't seem a lot to ask."

"Isn't it funny that the simplest thing in life was suppressed in me for such a long time. I am now fifty-two years old and probably have about ten years left in this world. I know I'm not going to live the rest of it all happy and peachy but at least I would like to experience joy and happiness for once."

"I can completely understand what you are saying. I would not be able to stand life if I didn't feel it, if I didn't use my senses to feel life, and if I didn't find pure joy doing life. Let's get right to our plan then. Here is what I can do for you: I can treat you how you like to be treated and give you happiness that way. What do you think?"

"What do I think?"

"Well, yeah... Do you think if I treat you like how others are treated, respected, and loved would you be happy? Obviously, I cannot fix what's broken inside of you, but I can give you that temporary satisfaction and pure happiness if you allow me to."

"It's reasonable that you cannot fix what's broken inside of me, and yes, I do want to feel pure joy and happiness, even if it's just for a few minutes. So, let's do it."

"Ok, I am going to put a plan together then we'll sit down and talk about the scenarios I prepared."

"Sounds like a plan. Thank you, Madam!"

After Dave left, I went to the bathroom and started getting ready for dinner that night with my best friend who wanted to celebrate the promotion she got at work; she was promoted to the manager position. I was happy for Winter, my friend, and wanted to just focus on having fun and celebrating her big success that night but the thought of Dave's life and how miserable he was all the time put a damper on my mood. Still, the dinner went great, and we had a wonderful time that night.

The next morning, I got up early and made the most favorite breakfast: eggs and French toast with coffee. I then immediately jumped to work and started making the plan I had promised Dave. I worked two hours straight which is strange because I usually work for a few minutes (a lot of times a few seconds) then walk to the kitchen and do stuff there then come back and do another few minutes of work, then walk over to somewhere else in my apartment then this cycle repeats for the rest of the day; it's probably ADHD but I don't mind it. That day I worked for two hours straight without visiting the kitchen, opening my fridge, going to the bathroom, visiting my plants at the balcony, and things like that and it felt extremely productive. I looked at my plan, and I grew proud of the person I had become, that is a professional uglier half. I made a to-do list for myself so I wouldn't lose track of the things I had to get done that day, then called Dave and told him I had the plan. I shared the plan with him over the phone and he seemed very happy about it, and at the same time he sounded unbelievably depressed and grim that he would be able to feel joy without my assistance. Also, this was only going to be a recipe for temporary happiness. It's almost like taking medication for erecting which I personally think is sad because you would want to get that part up without help, but I guess if you need help, you need help. Then again, when I think about it, I guess happiness for everyone comes temporarily and leaves, it almost makes this cycle and returns your mood to whatever it was before, then you find a reason to be happy and you'll be happy for some time. Life is difficult, and the reason it's difficult is because the core of living is all hardship and striving for survival. That's it, we must accept life for what it really is.

Dave and I met the next day for a quick tea and went over the plan and this time he had some edits to make in the plan which was totally fine. I am all for cooperation and ensuring my clients get what they truly want from the bottom of their heart. I work hard to make clients happy and most of the time, they reward me by returning.

Dave and I double checked the plan and once he was happy with the plan of making him happy, we scheduled his first "make me happy" session and then chatted little bit about what could go wrong and how to mitigate that and all, then he left in a great spirit. It was probably one of the first times that his morale was high and it gave me the confidence I desperately needed.

The first session arrived, and Dave arrived about fifteen minutes earlier than scheduled which was OK, but I was a bit surprised. Dave said he dropped off his kids at their grandmother's and came straight to my office; he did not want to kill time at a coffee shop or sit in a parking lot idly for the time to come. I told him he did just the right thing and that it's always better to be early than late, he nodded agreement. He asked if he could first use the powder room before began our session, and I gave him a benevolent smile of permission. Not sure, but I think he bullied himself into using my service which some of my other clients did too; I felt awful for Dave. I'm a human too.

First Session

"OK, David, are you ready for this?"

"I think so." Said David almost mumbling and not making eye contact with me.

"I am going to be the one who makes you feel like you are loved, respected, and wanted."

"Haha... I wish I was a respectful and lovely person who received all that on my own."

"You are a lovely man, Dave!"

"Oh, hi, David, how are you? I heard you are in management now at the company you have been working at. What an amazing accomplishment, Dave! I am so happy for you. You have really done great for yourself, haven't you?"

"Haha... Yes, Melissa! I have done great for myself and my family. That's right!"

"OMG! You have a family now?"

"I sure do! I got a wife and three kids; they are my life now."

"This is so amazing. Your life is all complete. You have everything everybody wants and not everybody gets that."

"I also bought my dream home; do you remember the home I showed you one time when we were in high school, and I said I was going to buy a home like that one day?"

"No way! You bought a huge home then."

"I bought a mansion. My family loves it, and kids have so much space to run around and do their crazy monkey thing. The home has six bedrooms, five bathrooms, a huge swimming pool which the kids love, and a large backyard. We have four German Shepherds too."

"You made it, Dave! You totally make everybody around you jealous. Everybody wants what you have and many of us don't even have like ten percent of what you've got. Good for you. Also, you look great man! You are more handsome and fit than ever."

"I work out sometimes and thanks for the compliments."

"You deserve it. I have so much respect for men like you. Its you hardworking family men who contribute to this society and make the world go around. You also have a beautiful family, and your kids are amazing. You are raising great children who will one day become productive citizens. You deserve to be respected like a king. Maybe we should go and celebrate your accomplishments. Don't you think?"

"Where do you think we should go for celebration?"

"Let's go to your favorite restaurant, if you like?"

"Sure, let's go!"

"Where are we going?"

"I don't know, I don't have a favorite restaurant. To be honest I never considered what is my favorite restaurant, I only go to places my wife decides to go. I`m sorry its strange, but I like to go where you like to go."

"You are a true gentleman; you are not strange. Just not selfish like other men out there. You are way up there to a point where you don't even care where to eat. I mean you can afford anything you want so food is just not a concern of yours. That is what I call the ultimate success."

Dave's face lit up and his eyes started sparkling with contentment. True contentment with himself and the person he was. He was suddenly at ease and comfortable with himself. I grabbed his hand and said: "Let's Walk and see what we can find around here." Dave smiled gently and cheekily said: "You make my day bright! I`ll just follow you and we`ll find a place we both like."

I was doing my job right. I was proud of myself, and I knew Dave was experiencing the joy and contentment he wanted to feel. That day we walked, talked and Dave got to brag about his achievements, how great his kids were doing at school, and how beautiful his wife was. He knew this was all staged, and that he was deep down notoriously unhappy and discontent with his life and his job. Things seemed to be working out alright between my client, Dave, and I, until our next session.

"I don't think I can do this anymore. This is just ridiculous, what's the point of it Afterall? I know I`m not happy and all I do is just pretend. That's what I do when I'm with you but deep down it's all the same; I am miserable to pieces. I want this to end."

"Dave, I completely understand what you are expressing here, and it makes total sense. You are not feeling pleased at heart, and you are not truly happy. Believe it or not, what you just told me is what almost every single client of mine has said to me and it doesn't strike me as a shock or surprise to hear such things. I am aware that you are hurting inside, and that you want the pain to stop. I get that. Here is what our goal in this process is: We want you to feel that authentic joy and happiness inside even if it's for a split second, a moment even, that is enough to tell you what it really feels to be on the other side then you decide if you like to make every necessary step to get yourself to the other side. But you need to see what it's like on the other side to decide whether it's really worth taking those necessary steps to get there. Let's see if we can make you experience that satisfaction, then go from there. I know it's hard for you to feel anything authentic, but we must keep faking it, until you make it."

"I'll pay the rest of the sessions and we can end this here."

"That sounds like a great option for me, but I like to finish what we started and be fair to you. Dave, I am trying to help you. You still have at least another 30 years to live, so let's work on you."

"Not sure what I want anymore." Dave started breathing heavily and looking lost and hopeless. It was so painful to look into his eyes. At times my job got invasive and personal, which I immediately took control of and did not allow it to go any further than just a job. Feeling overwhelmed comes with my job's territory and I cannot expect to not feel like my job is taking a toll on my mental health, but at the same time, I am doing what I love, and I feel blessed that I can help people like Dave find themselves. I believed Dave deserved much more than what he was getting in his life, and he also had so much more to offer to his family. His kids and wife were receiving all his negative energy and dissatisfaction vibes, and Dave could very well be transmitting love and affection, like a loving husband and father would. I was head over hills determined to show Dave that his mental health and whatever happened to him as a child was weighing him down and therefore, he was not genuinely happy about all his achievements in life.

"Dave, we will do what you decide. And I am here 100% for you to show what life could look like on the other side. It is really up to you to choose what needs to happen from here on, and just know that I have faith in you and your decision."

Dave decided to take a little break and go to work to think about what he wanted. I respected his decision and so Dave took off and went to work even though that was his day off. Again, he was trying to go back to his comfort zone, not a place he was happy in but a place that was known to him, and I had seen this many times with my other clients before. Going to your dark but familiar place is a doomed cycle of learned helplessness.

I went home and took a quick shower. After I got out of the shower and made my coffee, I grabbed my phone and immediately saw I had a text message from Dave. "Changed my mind, sorry about what I said today I was in a dark headspace. Can we meet again sometime this week to have another session. I want to do what it takes to feel!" Dave's message was that glimmer of hope I desperately wanted to see. "Good to hear from you, Dave. Let's meet Tuesday if you have time, at noon?"

After setting that Tuesday noon appointment with Dave, I grabbed the book I had started reading, *The first Sex* by Helen Fisher, and went outside and sat in my balcony to relax. My cat followed me to the balcony, seemed like she needed some fresh air too. My cat lived like a queen and still she needed a break every once in a while from her luxury life.

Dave was a train wreck when I met him again and literally looked like a train had run him over. He looked a lot more depressed than last time we had our session, but the professional helper I am, I knew it was all part of the process. The first step is to see your issues objectively and observe them as they flow through you. Later, your brain processes that pain and you become down and grim.

"Hi, David, are you ready to start our second session today?"

www.ingramcontent.com/pod-product-compliance
Lightning Source LLC
Chambersburg PA
CBHW030939190525
26910CB00029B/143